Gems

by Grace Hansen

abdopublishing.com

Published by Abdo Kids, a division of ABDO, PO Box 398166, Minneapolis, Minnesota 55439.

Copyright © 2016 by Abdo Consulting Group, Inc. International copyrights reserved in all countries. No part of this book may be reproduced in any form without written permission from the publisher.

Printed in the United States of America, North Mankato, Minnesota.

052015

092015

 THIS BOOK CONTAINS
RECYCLED MATERIALS

Photo Credits: iStock, Science Source, Shutterstock

Production Contributors: Teddy Borth, Jennie Forsberg, Grace Hansen

Design Contributors: Laura Rask, Dorothy Toth

Library of Congress Control Number: 2014958551

Cataloging-in-Publication Data

Hansen, Grace.

 Gems / Grace Hansen.

  p. cm. -- (Geology rocks!)

ISBN 978-1-62970-906-2

Includes index.

1. Gems--Juvenile literature. 2. Precious stones--Juvenile literature.   I. Title.

553.8--dc23

              2014958551

Table of Contents

What Makes a Gem?

Gemstones are rare. They are pretty. They are also strong.

4

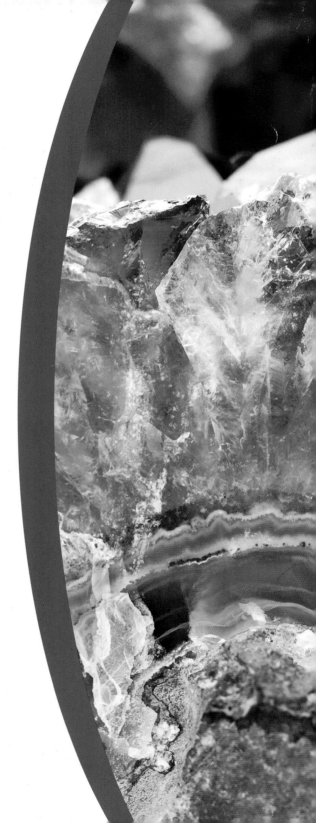

Most gems are **mineral** crystals. They form inside rocks. They can form in different ways.

11

Water Gems

Water can help form gems.

Water has **minerals** in it.

12

13

Many rocks are underwater.
Rocks on land are rained
on. **Minerals** in water seep
inside the rocks. Layers
of crystals form inside.

15

Magical Mollusks

Living things can make gems too! Oysters are **mollusks**. They can make pearls. Pearls are gems.

Tiny animals can enter oysters. Pieces of shell can enter them too.

19

Nacre builds up around the object. Nacre is smooth and shiny. This is how pearls are made.